NEW DAY, NEW START

NEW DAY, NEW START

#SEEKYOURSUNRISE

JEN CLARKE

Inspira

New Day, New Start: Seek Your Sunrise
First Edition Trade Book, 2021

To reach Jen, you can contact her through:
Email: jen.clarke.fi@gmail.com.
Website: www.seekyoursunrise.com

To order additional books:
www.amazon.com
www.seekyoursunrise.com

ISBN: 978-1-952943-09-6

Book Production: Inspira Literary Solutions, Gig Harbor, WA
Cover Design: Brianna Showalter
Typesetting: PerfecType, Nashville, TN

Printed in the USA

I dedicate this book to all the people who
are stuck in the transitions of life,
who want to reclaim joy, health, and
wellness that has been lost.
You are not alone!
I've got you!

CONTENTS

INTRODUCTION

This book is for people who want to improve the quality of their life through implementing simple tools of truth that transform the mind, reduce stress, and reclaim joy. In this book you will find simplicity—truths of change that start today.

Every day, every person in every moment has the power to choose the direction and focus of the thoughts, words, and behaviors that define their future. This takes deliberate and intentional focus in every area of life.

When we understand and accept that where we are today is a direct result of every choice we have made up to this very moment—the good, the bad, the ugly, the easy, the hard, the happy, the sad—we will find great power in accepting responsibility. We will also be empowered to create a future that is shaped by the positive choices we make today. We may not be able to control our circumstances, but we absolutely control how we *respond* to our circumstances. We get to choose the lens through which we see our life, our future, and our destiny.

I wrote this book because I believe strongly that each day is a new day—a new start—to live a renewed life. We must choose to believe that, each day, we start with a clean slate, a new opportunity to start fresh.

In the following pages, you will read what I believe are tools of truth that support the power of choice. These are truths and wisdom I have learned and embraced through many avenues, including my education (BA Psychology, M. Ed Counseling), the Bible, Native American philosophies, Christian leaders, contemporary authors, and professional athletes. My education, certifications, study, and service—gathered over 25 years through my work as a high school counselor, a varsity athletics head coach, a non-profit community service volunteer, and a Federal Corrections Case Manager—have guided my precepts.

I hope you will read the words with personal application in mind, and reflect on how they speak to you.

HOW TO USE THIS BOOK

This book is designed to be used interactively as you read through the chapters. The idea is that when you actively absorb content (the **"Meditate"** section of each chapter), followed by answering prompted questions or completing recommended action steps (the **"Activate"** section), and then reading inspiring thoughts, challenges, and quotes that reflect that chapter (the **"Ruminate"** section), the concepts will be embedded into your awareness more deeply than if you were to just read straight information.

In each chapter, there will be opportunities for you to think critically and reflectively, to self-assess and journal, and to set goals and aspirations for yourself. I hope you will not just brush past these sections, but will go slowly and methodically enough through each one, absorbing its content and following the directions. My hope is that you can let this book be an opportunity for you to take what speaks to you personally and implement it into your day, your week, and even your life.

I am excited for this journey for you. Are you ready? Then get set. Now, GO!!!

CHAPTER *One*

THE POWER OF DAILY RENEWAL

MEDITATE

Every day, every person in every moment has the power to choose the direction and focus of their thoughts, behavior, and attitude. It takes deliberate intention to pay attention to thoughts, hold them captive, and align them to the truth. It forces us to slow down and be fully present, constantly aware of our inner dialogue. We must fight the urge to hurry. We must fight the world's idea that we don't have the time to slow down. "Life is too busy," society tells us. The truth is that life is as busy as we choose to make it. Choose to slow down your thoughts, steady your mindset, and listen to your inner dialogue. There is great power in being still, which includes prayer, meditation, and contemplation.

To transform your mind and renew your life, it will require you to make deliberate choices every day. This means adjusting thoughts, habits, priorities, and actions. You can do it!

How you start your day is an imperative part of this process. I call this "daily renewal." Every morning, you have the opportunity to view your life as a fresh, clean slate. Starting with your very first thoughts, you can choose to launch yourself into a positive mindset or a negative one. You get to choose—it's your call!

The power of daily renewal begins with a positive lens to approach the day ahead. Yesterday is behind you. Tomorrow is beyond you. All you have is today, this very moment. I encourage you to make it amazing and **#SeekYourSunrise**!

With that in mind, here are some simple tools that will help guide you into a most meaningful, purposeful, and powerful start to your day.

The Joy-Filled Life

> *"Finally brothers and sisters, whatever is true, whatever is honorable, whatever is just, whatever is lovely, whatever is commendable, if there is any excellence, if there is anything worthy of praise, think about these things."* **Philippians 4:8, ESV**

What we put into our minds determines what comes out in our words and actions. The book by life coach Tommy Newberry, *The 4:8 Principle: The Secret to a Joy-Filled Life,* speaks to the fact that life is a mixture of good and bad, positive and negative, and we always have things to complain about and things that bring us joy. Helpful thinking and destructive thinking are merely habits that we have created and practiced over time. We can train ourselves to think about things that *produce* joy and peace, rather than waiting for joy and peace to come and find us. Here are some examples:

negative thinking:

- "I am so sad; I am never going to find joy again."
- "Things will never change."
- "This will never work."
- "I am not capable of being loved."

positive thinking:

- "I know I can achieve this."
- "Life is going to be a blessing."
- "I am worth it."
- "I can make the best of this."

Seek out truth in criticism. What can you gain in building your wisdom and character through such information (whether or not you like it)? Then, *throw out* whatever does not build you up, and *keep* what makes you stronger.

Newberry states that the most effective technique for installing the habit of the 4:8 principle thinking is developing the habit of asking, re-asking, and answering the following five questions:

1. What are five things I am grateful/thankful for right now?
2. What are five of my biggest strengths or positive traits?
3. What are five of my best achievements so far?
4. Who are the five people who love me most?
5. What five things am I looking forward to in the next seven days?

These questions will put you in a positive frame of mind. They will actually change your biochemistry and give you renewed energy and confidence. I encourage you to start your day asking yourself and answering these five questions—before you take your first step out of bed!

Since practice makes perfect and developing habits requires repetition, the following pages will provide you space to think through and answer the above five questions. Take your time and be thoughtful and intentional.

"Don't let what you **CANNOT** do interfere with what you *can* do!" **ARTHUR ASH**

ACTIVATE

First thing in the morning, ask yourself the following:

What are the *five* things I am grateful/thankful for right now?

1. ______________________________
2. ______________________________
3. ______________________________
4. ______________________________
5. ______________________________

What are *five* of my strengths/positive traits?

1. ______________________________
2. ______________________________
3. ______________________________
4. ______________________________
5. ______________________________

What are *five* of my best achievements so far?

1. ______________________________
2. ______________________________
3. ______________________________
4. ______________________________
5. ______________________________

Who are *five* people who love/support me most?

1. ________________________________
2. ________________________________
3. ________________________________
4. ________________________________
5. ________________________________

What are *five* things I am looking forward to in the next seven days?

1. ________________________________
2. ________________________________
3. ________________________________
4. ________________________________
5. ________________________________

It is important to deliberately and intentionally start your day integrating BALANCE into your life. This means that you implement activity in the five elements of the human condition. These elements spell the acronym S.P.I.E.S. (I will speak more to this concept in greater detail in Chapter 3.)

S: Spiritual
P: Physical
I: Intellectual
E: Emotional
S: Social

DO WHAT
YOU CAN TO
BECOME A
better,
STRONGER
YOU.

Next, answer the following:

What can I do today to connect with my *spirit*?

1. ______________________________
2. ______________________________
3. ______________________________

What can I do today to move my body, feed my body, and nurture my *body*?

1. ______________________________
2. ______________________________
3. ______________________________

What can I do today to engage my mind/body *intellectually*?

1. ______________________________
2. ______________________________
3. ______________________________

What can I do today to honor my *emotions* and handle any challenging conversation in a healthy way?

1. ______________________________
2. ______________________________
3. ______________________________

With whom will I connect *socially* today, bringing me joy, encouragement, and laughter?

1. ______________________________
2. ______________________________
3. ______________________________

RUMINATE

Each day, we get to start with a fresh, clean slate in our mind, thoughts, attitude, and behavior. We get to choose, from the very first moment we wake up, if we will be grateful for another day or if we will dread the early alarm. We can choose to embrace gratitude for a job we *get* to go to and the people we *get* to impact, or begrudge the job we *have* to go to and the people we *must* get along with. Are we going to exercise and feed our body nutritious food or are we going to sleep in, skip the exercise, and grab a sugary donut? Whatever we choose, we own it: the good, the bad, the ugly. No excuses. It sets us up for our tomorrow. Be the best YOU that you can be . . . to bring light to those that surround you, to give hope for the kingdom to come (see Matthew 5:16).

Make it a great day and be a blessing to others!

CHAPTER *Two*

THE POWER OF WORDS, THOUGHTS, AND MENTAL DIALOGUE

MEDITATE

Words, thoughts, and our ongoing mental dialogue have the power to change our biochemistry, including our heart rate, our hormones, our attitude, and our entire state of awareness.

As you read in Chapter 1, "The Power of Daily Renewal," we start each morning with a clean, clear mind that we get to fill with whatever we want. In those exercises and concepts, I provided you with some fuel to put your mind into action with positive intent.

Here, in Chapter 2, I will break down how important it is to answer those questions with intentional, deliberate, and powerful words. When put together with the inner work you did in Chapter 1, it can create a powerful thought. This can be the catalyst to completely change your inner voice.

When we train ourselves to use positive, powerful, and intentional words that bring encouragement, guidance, and love to every life conversation, we will notice a dramatic shift in every relationship we have (with ourselves, others, God, and the world around us). After all, life really "is all about relationship"—with God, with family, with friends, with enemies, with nature, with creatures, with money, with death, and more. If we can learn how to practice control over our words—only speaking words and thoughts that bring encouragement and truth to all our relationships—what joy and fulfillment we would experience in life!

With all that in mind, let's spend some time thinking about words. If you could replace every negative word with a positive word that could give the same message, it would turn that conversation from an attacking, fault-finding, and destructive connection into an encouraging, guiding, constructive connection. This is true whether it is your own self-talk or how you speak to those around you. If the way you speak about yourself in your own mind is attacking, fault-finding, and destructive, how do you feel about you?

What if you started your practice of using these powerful and uplifting words by focusing on whom God created you to be and the gifts with which you've been blessed? See how that impacts your desire to honor and respect who and what you are, even with all that is imperfect. You will likely shift your lens to accept those imperfections and turn them into personal learning opportunities.

Then, once you experience this powerful process over your own self-talk, look at all the relationships you have around you, and implement the same process.

"We do not attract that which we *want*, but rather that which we *are*."

—JAMES ALLEN

ACTIVATE

Taking Charge of Your Mind

Following are some quotes directly from Joyce Meyer's book, *The Battlefield of the Mind.*[1] Take some time to ponder them:

We have the power to control our thoughts and therefore choose the health of our mind.

We can choose sinful nature of the flesh or live according (in accordance) to the Spirit (see Galatians 5:22-23).

The mind controlled by the Spirit is a life of peace (see Romans 7:14-15).

Take time to think about . . . what you are thinking about.

---

1. Meyer, Joyce, and Joyce Meyer. *Battlefield of the Mind: Winning the Battle in Your Mind.* New York: Faith Words, 2017.

A negative mind = A negative life

A positive mind = A positive life

You cannot have a positive life and a negative mind.

Your life will not get straightened out until your mind does.

It is easy to quit; it takes faith to go through.

It takes PRACTICE! Practice, practice, practice and re-do, re-do, re-do—along with with replace, replace, replace!

Every Negative → Positive

Every Attack → Embrace

Every Destructive → Constructive

Every Curse → Blessing

Take time to process your words, thoughts, and mindset in a quiet, private place. Really slow down, ponder, and meditate on:

- each and every word used in a sentence
- on what sentence comes next
- on what end result and message you want to deliver
- on how that message will impact your relationship . . .

    with you,

        with others,

            with the future.

I encourage you to process through writing, running, hiking, or any other means that is meditative and involves only you and your thoughts.

We must start with the end in mind. What kind of relationship do you want to have at the end of the conversation? Will you have this person in your life every day? Every week? Every month? Every year? Sometime in the future? And when you see that person again, how will the end of this current conversation impact the next "run-in?"

Take the *care*

To take the *time*

To make it *right*

The first *time . . .*

The Toltec Indian "Four Agreements"

1. Be impeccable with your word.
2. Don't take anything personally.
3. Don't make assumptions (assume positive intent).
4. Always do your best.

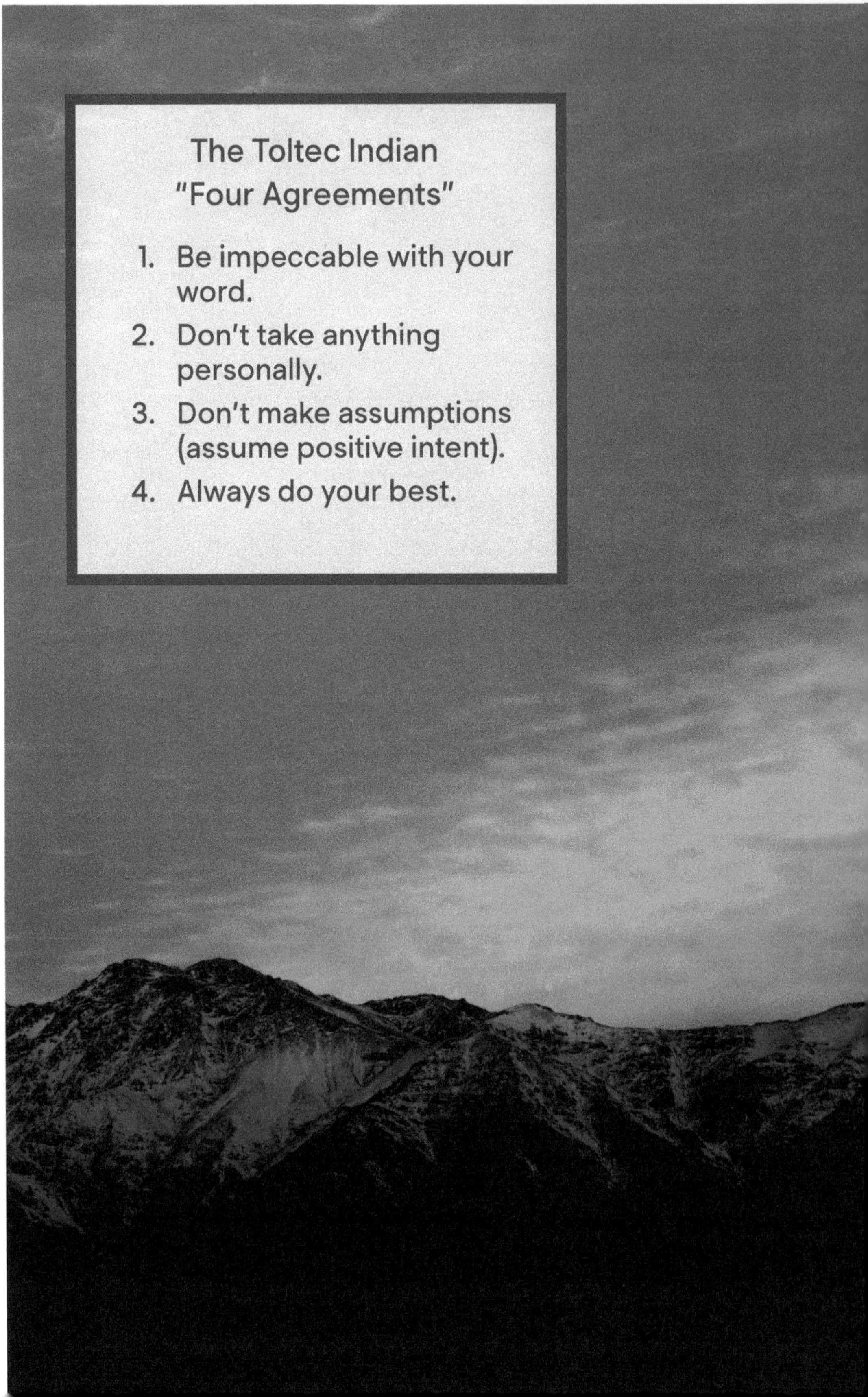

ACTIVATE

Think of a current situation in your life in which a difficult conversation is ahead of you. Determine what type of relationship you want to have with this person at the end of the conversation. This will dictate how you address him or her. If this person in your life will be with you down the road, use the Toltec Indian Four Agreements to guide your words and attitude in that conversation. Write down each sentence and align it to the agreement. At the end of the Four Agreements, reflect on how that conversation feels when you are finished.

On the next few pages, you will find blank lines for you to record your thoughts, impressions, intentions, and experiences related to the Four Agreements and how you applied them to your relationships.

"The wise person speaks frugally. The tongue rightly used can nourish or feed others. A compliment or word of encouragement can brighten someone's outlook or motivate a person to pursue a dream."[2]

2. Barker, Kenneth L., and John R. Kohlenberger. *Zondervan NIV Bible Commentary.* Zondervan Pub. House, 1994.

Be *Impeccable* with Your Word

Only use your words to encourage and to guide. Otherwise, say nothing—just listen!

Don't Take Anything *Personally*

Don't ever take anything another person says or does to you personally. It is not about YOU. It is a reflection of their own reality and lens through which they see life. You do not know what that person has experienced in their life, nor do you know what has happened in the last five, 10, 30, or 60 minutes.

Allow others to express their inner heart, and if it is dark, reflect light. If it is hurtful, reflect love. If it is bitter, jealous, angry, or resentful, then be the example of using your words to encourage and guide.

"BY CHANGING MY *belief* I CHANGE WHO I *am*."
—JAMES ALLEN

Don't Make *Assumptions*

Do not make any judgments. Ask questions and be clear with your intent. Discover, search, and seek the truth of the matter.

Always Do Your Best

Be the best you that you can be no matter what the day brings you. Do your best on that day. Some days your best will look different than other days. If you are sick, hurt, or troubled, do your best with where you are, and whatever you've got.

RUMINATE

Words are singularly the most powerful force available to humanity. We can choose to use this force constructively with words of encouragement, or destructively using words of criticism or despair. Physical reality is an energetic system; remember, your thoughts are energy. You create manifestations through thoughts, words, and actions that use energy to form objects, conditions, experiences, and outcomes. Now that is some power! Think of a meditation journey.[3]

Words, too, have energy and power, with the ability to help and to heal, or to hinder, hurt, humiliate, and humble. According to Andrew Newberg, MD, and Robert Waldman, words can literally change your brain. Positive words such as "peace" and "love" can alter the expression of genes, strengthening an area in our frontal lobes and promoting the brain's cognitive functioning.[4]

This ability to use our thoughts and words to create not only a new attitude but an entire mindset and even physiological change in our bodies has been called a "growth mindset" by author Carol Dweck in her book *Mindset*.[5] The definition of a growth mindset is: "the belief that our basic abilities, intelligence, and talents are fixed traits (fixed mindset) versus the belief that abilities and intelligence can be developed with effort, learning, and persistence (growth mindset)." To cultivate a growth mindset, you will need to consider the following mental internal dialogue (or something like it):

---

3. www.theteachingsofjoshua.com

4. www.psychcentral.com

5. Dweck, Carol S. *Mindset: Changing the Way You Think to Fulfil Your Potential*. London: Robinson, 2017.

"Do what you *know* is the right thing to do—even when no one is looking."

"Do what is right—because it's the right thing to do."

Remember:

- Your word is powerful; make it impeccable.
- Use your words wisely (sparingly), and with plenty of thoughtfulness.
- Always use your words to encourage and guide, never to harm or hurt.
- Your word can bring life or death—choose life.
- Your word can bless or curse—choose blessing.
- Your thoughts determine your words.
- Your words determine your behavior.
- Your behavior determines your habits.
- Your habits determine your character.
- Your character determines your future.
- Your future determines your destiny.
- Your thoughts, therefore, determine your destiny.

"Our *tongue* (words) does not affect only our *destiny*—it can also change the destiny of those we bless."

YOUR LIFE
WILL NOT GET
STRAIGHTENED
OUT UNTIL YOUR
MIND DOES.
—JOYCE MEYER

CHAPTER *Three*

THE POWER OF A BALANCED LIFE

(PART 1)

MEDITATE

Why is having balance in life important? What makes it so powerful?

There are seasons in our life when it seems, suddenly, we feel "stuck." We just cannot move forward and have somehow lost momentum. We feel uncomfortable—filled with tension, anxiety, and worry. We feel lost in our next step. We are worn out.

It is frustrating when we feel like our wheels are spinning. Not only are we not moving forward and growing in our potential, but sometimes, we slide backwards. Usually, this feeling occurs at a transition point in life. We are trying to close one chapter and struggling to figure out what we want the next chapter to entail. Or, sometimes, we have been living in a rut, a predictable routine, day in and day out, that has gone on for months, or even years. We realize: *Where is my joy? Where is my happiness? What am I doing? I need something to change!*

Here is where Life Balance is important. To get "unstuck," we need to reflect on five significant elements of the human condition essential in maintaining a healthy lifestyle. We need *balance*. We need to reflect and take control of how we address each element and make the decision to implement healthy choices. It is a *powerful* life tool.

As we saw earlier, the five elements of the human condition spell the acronym S.P.I.E.S.:

S: Spiritual
P: Physical
I: Intellectual
E: Emotional
S: Social/Community

In this chapter, we will address the first two elements—the SPIRITUAL and the PHYSICAL—and learn how to reflect and decide if we have been giving that element the time, effort, and energy it needs on a regular basis. Where there has been neglect, there is imbalance (disparity, variance, polarity). Tension is generated by imbalance.

Spiritual

We are spiritual creatures. In fact, we are spiritual first, then we are human. When our spirit leaves the body, the body dies. Our spirit continues to live. Energy cannot be created nor destroyed, therefore, our energy goes somewhere. That is proven science! This piece of who we are is vital to our very existence. Therefore, we need to connect with it on a regular basis. So, how do we connect with our spirit?

DO YOUR **BEST** EVERY DAY, WHATEVER THAT DAY BRINGS YOU IN YOUR HEALTH. SOMETIMES, THAT JUST MAY BE REST!

Here are some questions to consider:

- Do you have a faith?
- Were you raised in a religion?
- Did you or do you struggle with that upbringing?
- Do you have a spiritual leader, advisor, or mentor?
- Do you have access to that person?
- Do you spend time in prayer and meditation?
- Do you live according to your belief system?
- Do you study your faith?
- Do you enjoy weekly gatherings with those who share your faith?

You *must* spend time nurturing your spiritual element, growing it, and developing it. If you do not have a faith or a spiritual belief, then you are in a state of spiritual unawareness. Do not despair. What you have before you is an incredible opportunity for discovery. I encourage you to take a spiritual journey and seek *truth*. What you seek you will find. That is promised to all of us. What you believe matters. It determines the very placement of your spiritual energy when it leaves your body forever.

When you nurture your spirit here in this life, it gives you the opportunity to see all that surrounds you with a spiritual lens, such as a deeper sense of creation, an intense gratitude for beauty, nature, weather, and more. It basically allows you to appreciate the ebb and flow of every season—not to mention an eternal perspective.

I caution you: make sure you always seek that which is good, pure, honest, and true. Otherwise, if you seek darkness, you will find darkness. Remember, what you seek will eventually surround you. Your eyes will be opened one way or another. You have the power to choose the lens through which you see life.

Choose spiritual truth, choose goodness, and choose life.

Physical

Our physical self-care has many components. We need to address this in order to make sure we are caring for it in the best manner possible. We have power and control over every choice we make—how we nurture our physical condition and in how we honor our limitations. Here we will look at three components of physical nature:

- Exercise
- Nutrition
- Self-Care

Exercise: How do you move your body on a daily basis?

- Three types of movement:
  - Cardiovascular: Aerobic/Anaerobic
  - Strength/Conditioning
  - Stretching/Flexibility
  - Rest
- Why we need to move our body:
  - "If you don't move it, you lose it."
  - Circulation
  - Immediate shift in biochemistry and hormones
  - Synovial fluid movement and joint health
  - Bone density
  - Digestive health/mobilization
  - Mental health
  - Stress reduction

- Brain health
- Release of toxins
- Mind/body connection (Spirit tool)

Nutrition: How do you nourish your body every day?

- Our body responds to every single thing we put in our mouth.
- Feed it healthy, living food.
- Drink water (pure, filtered if possible). Our body is 70 percent water. Replenish often.
- Food is our body's most powerful drug.
- Nutrition and diet affects 80 percent of our weight.
- Exercise affects 10 percent of weight.
- Stay away from packaged food as much as possible (e.g., avoid food with additives, preservatives, chemicals, etc.—can you pronounce the ingredients?)
- Organize your refrigerator and pantry to have healthy food easily accessible. Get rid of junk.
- Plan your weekly menu—pre-cut and pre-cook when possible for convenience.

Self-care: How do you honor your body?

- Take regular hot Epsom salt baths/hot tub.
- Take regular saunas/steam (when possible).
- Shower daily and after exercise.
- Exfoliate skin.
- Seek regular dental care.
- Take care of your nails.
- Moisturize skin with essential oils and lotions.
- Employ positive body talk:
    - Speak words of gratitude over your entire body.
    - Appreciate what each body part does for you (start with your toes and work all the way up to your hair).

- When you exercise, speak gratitude for movement.
- Focus on what you like about your body.
- Where are you strong and powerful?
- Focus on what you *can* do!
- Set positive goals.
- Give yourself some grace!

"Start where you are.

Use what you have.

Do what you can!"

—ARTHUR ASH

Remember: if you declare war on your body, your body will fight back at you. Instead, declare gratitude, embrace change, and watch your body come alive in all that it is meant to be—in this season, in this moment, in this very breath.

ACTIVATE

In this chapter, your "activate" will be implementing the SPIRITUAL and PHYSICAL components we've just discussed. I've provided space for notes for you to set your own goals, and to be able to refer back to them to see how you're doing.

Spiritual Goals:

1.

2.

3.

4.

5.

Physical Goals:

1.

2.

3.

4.

5.

PHYSICAL

Your body is the temple of the Holy Spirit . . .

Respect it.
Nourish it.
Move it.
Strengthen it.
Be kind to it.
Appreciate it.
Be grateful for it.
Listen to it.

RUMINATE

Following are some self-assessment prompts to help you reflect on the material you've just read, and apply it to your own situation:

Physical

1. What will I do today to *move* my body? (e.g., walk, run, bike, strength train, stretch)

2. How will I *practice* nourishing my body? (e.g., What life-giving food will I eat? How can I monitor my water intake to make sure I'm getting at least eight glasses a day? How can I organize my refrigerator to make healthy food easily accessible?)

3. What *three* things will I do this week to honor my body? (e.g., eating habits, self-care, positive self-talk, pampering—like an Epsom salt bath, sauna, facial, etc.)

Physically, what can you start right now? What can you do today to set up for your tomorrow? Take at least *one* answer from each of the above questions. Record them below, along with your action steps that will help you make each one happen.

FAITH IN GOD

1. God is who He says He is.
2. God will do what He says He will do.
3. You are who God says you are.
4. You can do all things through Jesus Christ.
5. God is alive and active in me.[1]

---

1. Moore, Beth. *Believing God.* Nashville, TN: LifeWay Press, 2002.

Spiritual

1. Where do I find Truth?

2. What is the foundation of my moral compass? (How do I define right and wrong?)

3. Do I practice what I believe? What does that look like in my relationships and interactions with others? (e.g., with God, my family, my work setting, my friends, the checkout person at the grocery store)

4. Where do I see God's fingerprint in my surroundings?

5. Do I spend time mediating or contemplating my faith/ belief? When and where do I do this?

Reflect on your answers above and think through what you can start today to seek a stronger faith and relationship with God. What can you do right now? What can be your next steps for tomorrow?

CHAPTER *Four*

THE POWER OF A BALANCED LIFE

(PART 2)

MEDITATE

Intellectual

The third aspect of a balanced life—the "I" in S.P.I.E.S.—is paying attention to our intellect. Our mind and our intellect are powerful attributes of the entire human system. Our mind and thoughts actually dictate the entire chemical energy and hormonal distribution in our body. Think of the fight, flight, or freeze response.

Our intellect is stimulated and produces new neuron connections when we learn a new skill or when we study. This is amplified when we connect that knowledge to human performance and implement the skill learned into our daily lives.

We must be lifelong learners to keep our brains alive. It's not just about implementing what we already know; it is about being creative in learning new ways to approach life, opportunities, and obstacles.

- Make sure to challenge your brain.
  - Intellectually
  - Mathematically
  - Scientifically
  - Theoretically
  - Theologically
  - Interpersonally
- Read, listen to podcasts, watch video productions, etc. Learn through all of your senses.
- Take a class in which you are required to memorize material to pass the course.
- Learn a new skill and test it.
  - Martial arts
  - Dancing
  - Race car driving
  - Solo sky diving
  - Music (learn a new instrument)
  - Voice lessons, choral singing, join a musical group or theater
  - Art (painting, drawing, sculpting)
  - Woodworking, gardening
- Make sure to pay attention to your internal dialogue.
  - Are you positive?
  - Are you critical?
  - Do you believe you can learn difficult material?
  - Do you "give up" when you "don't get it?"
  - Does fear paralyze your progress?
  - Do you have an "I have not learned it . . . yet!!" attitude?
- Remember:

  Embrace a *growth mindset.*

  A positive mind = a **positive** life.

  A negative mind = a **negative** life.

  It is your *choice.*

GET WISDOM

Wisdom is knowledge put into practice. Wisdom does not exist if it is not living, breathing action. Get wisdom, treasure it, and implement it into every fabric of your being. It will guide you into that which is pleasing to God. (Hint: For a great source of life wisdom—#lifehacks—check out the Book of Proverbs in the Bible!)

Emotional

Fourthly, we are designed to be emotional creatures. Emotions are healthy—both ones that feel good and ones that feel heavy. However, we must be able to express our emotions in such a way that it does not negatively impact, impede, or hurt those around us. Therefore, it is essential we obtain tools that we can access and utilize in order to express our emotions in a healthy and positive way.

- Take some time and reflect on what you do when you are angry, sad, upset. What do others see?
- Do you go to a private place to emote?
- Do you engage in a physical activity to release energy? (e.g., run, walk, bike, shoot hoops, workout, etc.)
- Do you listen to music?
- Do you journal?
- Do you talk with a counselor/therapist/mentor?
- Do you have friends you can reach out to and process the situation calmly?
- How do you approach a difficult conversation?
  - Do you think through your words before you speak?
  - Do you keep the end in mind . . . in how you want the relationship to stand?
  - Do you use words that encourage and guide with positive intent?

It is always best to take time to think through an emotional situation before you say or do anything. Take time to get yourself calm first. Then, think through how you want to handle the situation. Let yourself be honest. When you find yourself contemplating words of condemnation, negativity, or hurtfulness, STOP! Breathe. Remember to use only words of encouragement or guidance. Then, try the internal conversation again, and again, and again—until you feel good about what your lens will be when the opportunity comes to engage in that hard conversation. You will be glad you took the time to process your words, your heart, your attitude, and the lens through which you honor your character and your relationships.

Social

The final component of the S.P.I.E.S. acronym for a balanced life is "social." It is vital that we have a healthy and consistent connection to our social being and community at large. We are designed to be in relationship. We are not designed to be alone and isolated—by nature, we are social beings. We need to have time with friends, family, community, and also private time to ourselves. It is a balancing act. We need all of it. So, make sure when reflecting on your social life you are spending time with the following:

- Family
- Friends (two to three close relationships)
- Community (organizations you believe in and ones that "fill your cup")
- Charity

It is great to volunteer at local organizations where you meet people with similar passions and interests. It is also important to join clubs that meet regularly to participate in an activity and/or hobby that you enjoy (this also is an intellectually stimulating pursuit). Attend conferences on subjects that ignite your enthusiasm for helping others.

Remember, every day is a gift, an opportunity to be a blessing to someone else! An opportunity to be a positive light in a world with so much sadness. Loving people love on others. Hurting people hurt others.

And, a last note: when looking at your life, as you reflect on your daily routine, take note of what you believe is your number one top value in life—and make sure it is also your top priority. You must put first what is first, every day.

When your priorities and habits do not align with your values, you will not be in a healthy, balanced place. For example, if you say to others, "I value family first; it is my number one priority," but you seem to be at the office 24/7 (missing family meals, events, traditions, etc.) then you are not in alignment. You get to decide where, how, and with whom you spend your time based on what you prioritize. You decide. It's a choice.

ACTIVATE

Answer the following in the spaces provided:

What are *five* things you can learn that excite you and intellectually challenge/stimulate your brain?

1. ______________________________
2. ______________________________
3. ______________________________
4. ______________________________
5. ______________________________

List *five* ways you can process your emotions without impacting or hurting others:

1. ____________________
2. ____________________
3. ____________________
4. ____________________
5. ____________________

List *five* things you can do to get socially connected to friends and your community:

1. ____________________
2. ____________________
3. ____________________
4. ____________________
5. ____________________

RUMINATE

Our life is meant to be lived purposefully. What we do here, on this earth, matters. Our mind, our emotions, and our social relationships are meant to be developed, to grow, to maximize the potential within.

What are you passionate about? What do you love learning about? What fills your heart with joy? What impact do you want to have on your community? Write down your answers to these questions and ponder what you can do today. What can you start right now? What can you prepare today to launch into your tomorrow?

CHAPTER *Five*

THE POWER OF PRIORITIES

MEDITATE

What you value first (most) must *be* first every day! Priorities matter. Period.

Your priorities—the top-to-bottom list of what is important to you in your life defines your construct of daily living. It determines what you put first every single day. It determines what you say "yes" to and what you say "no" to. Priorities determine your actions, your habits, and your character.

That being said, your values comprise the heart center of what you believe in—a standard of behavior, one's judgment of what is important in life (spiritually, physically, intellectually, emotionally, and socially). Your values help to prioritize the list of everything you do, every day.

Your values and your priorities must be in alignment to obtain a joy-filled and satisfied life. When our values do not align with our priorities, our mind, body, and soul will experience tension, imbalance, anxiety, a lack of purpose—or even failure.

A priority is something that changes due to outside influences and demands. A value is something outside influences cannot change. This is why I say, "Priorities matter." What you put first must *actually* be first every day. In other words, practice what you preach. Here are some examples of what happens when your priorities and values are not in alignment:

Scenario #1:

- You say that your family is your priority—yet you are constantly missing out on family time by working extra hours.
- You find that you've missed family events, your children's performances or games, even dinner at home with the family.
- You begin to notice you're tense when you get a call at work and are asked if you're going to make it to your child's soccer game, band concert, ballet recital, etc. and you know you will not be there due to appointments, deadlines, meetings, and other work-related things.
- You think, *How can I pay all the bills at home and afford all the athletic gear, instruments, and lessons? I must work harder, longer, and take on more opportunities that will advance my career . . .*

A *choice* is in the horizon.
A **decision** is in the near future.

You must recognize that what you say is a priority (your family) is not where you are choosing to spend your time. You *value* your family, but work is the *priority*. Therefore, you must either change your priority or change your value to reduce the daily angst, tension, and frustration that lingers in your body, mind, and spirit. What you put first but be first every day.

Scenario #2:

If you say, "God comes first in my life," but you have not picked up your Bible, devotional, or rosary in weeks. You've not prayed. You've not gathered with other believers for encouragement and support and worship. *Is He first?* Is He a priority in your daily habits?

Tell me what you do every day, and I will tell you what your priorities are. Whether you like it or not, where you spend your time is where your priorities rest.

Make sure you value your list of priorities. When determining your priorities, it is helpful to look at your value construct. What do you value in life? What matters most? Throughout this book you will find various words of wisdom from authors, athletes, gurus, and Christian thought leaders that can help guide you in the exercise of defining your values and setting your priorities. Choose the truths that speak to you. Keep a journal. Make a list. Determine your priorities and begin to practice your priorities (in alignment with your values) in each and every day.

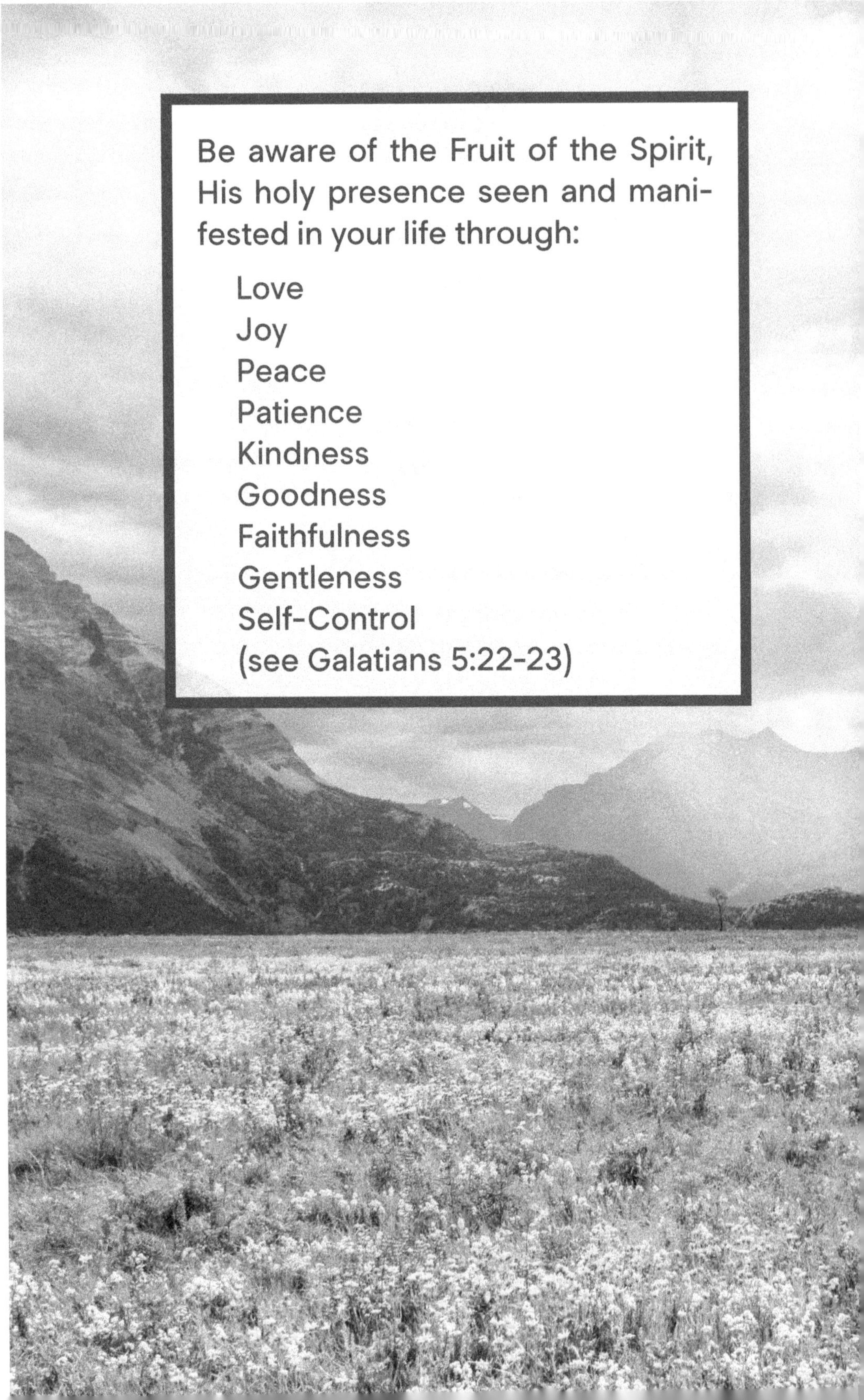

Be aware of the Fruit of the Spirit, His holy presence seen and manifested in your life through:

Love
Joy
Peace
Patience
Kindness
Goodness
Faithfulness
Gentleness
Self-Control
(see Galatians 5:22-23)

ACTIVATE

List your top *five* priorities (things that you put first today):

1. ______________________________
2. ______________________________
3. ______________________________
4. ______________________________
5. ______________________________

List *five* things you value most in your life:

1. ______________________________
2. ______________________________
3. ______________________________
4. ______________________________
5. ______________________________

Ask yourself, "How am I doing at making sure I am prioritizing the things I value? Is there anything I need to re-evaluate? What is my joy factor?" Use the space provided below to write your responses.

____

____

____

____

____

____

____

____

RUMINATE

Read the thoughts and quotes below and ponder how they impact your priorities and values:
What is *"pleasing"* to God?

- To love God with all your heart, mind, soul, and strength
- To love your neighbor as yourself (see Mark 12:30-31).

What is *love*?

- Love is an action word.
- Love is doing what you know is right and pleasing to God.

It is:

1. Feeding the hungry
2. Clothing those without clothes
3. Helping and caring for the widows and orphans
4. Using your words to bless others
5. Visiting those in prison
6. Using your God-given talent to bring joy and pleasure to those around you
7. If you have been given a blessing—a gift—from God, using that blessing or gift to build His kingdom

What is a *blessing* or *gift* from God?

1. Caring for your family (your spouse, children, grandchildren—for they are gifts from God)
2. Financial success gained from hard work, commitment, and God-given opportunity
3. Musical talent in voice and instrument
4. Artistic talent in all mediums

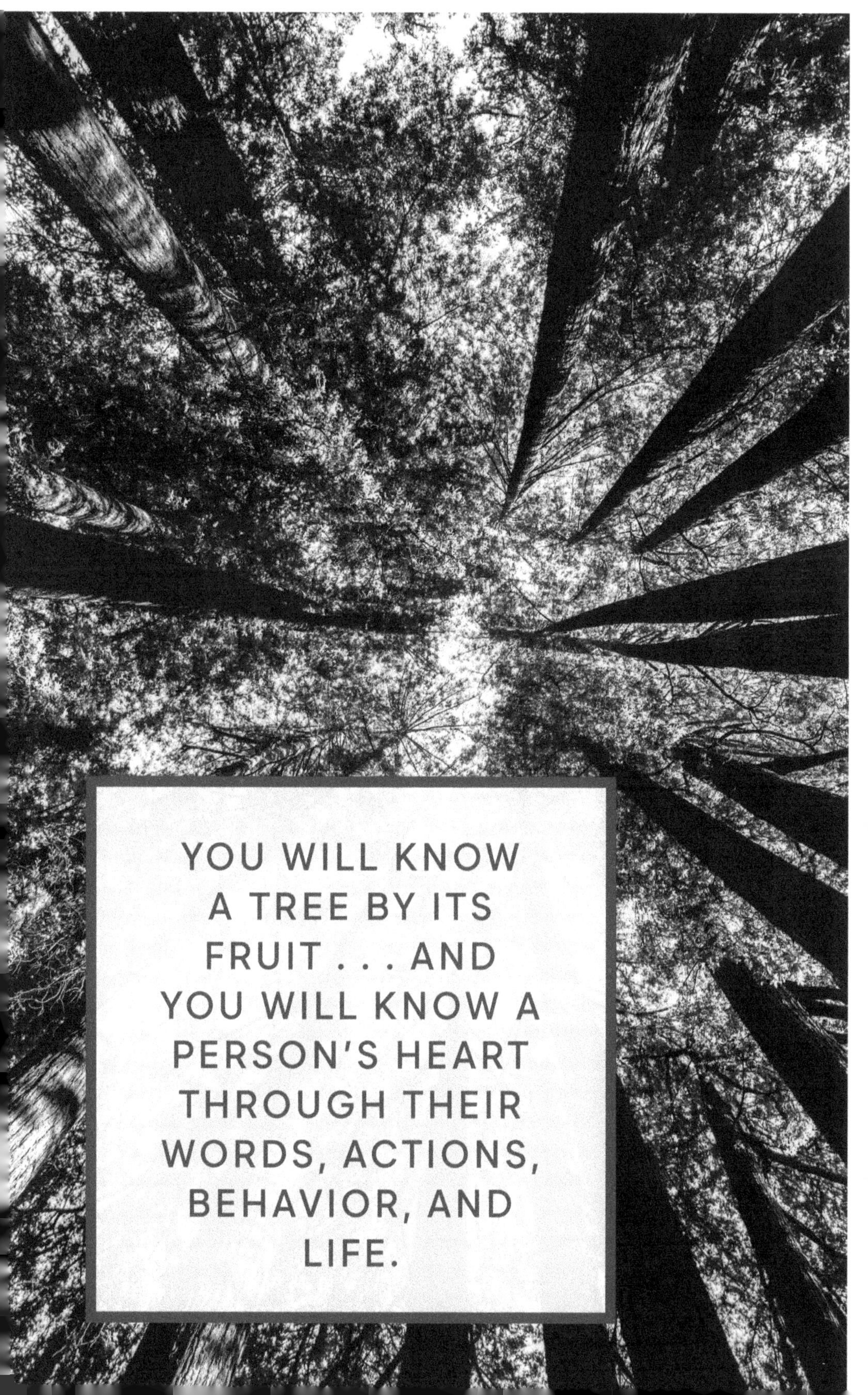
YOU WILL KNOW A TREE BY ITS FRUIT . . . AND YOU WILL KNOW A PERSON'S HEART THROUGH THEIR WORDS, ACTIONS, BEHAVIOR, AND LIFE.

5. Intellectual talent to increase knowledge
6. The ability to encourage, motivate, teach, counsel, instruct—to bring hope
7. Spiritual gifts, such as prophecy, speaking in tongues, preaching, missions, intercession
8. Athletic prowess
9. Any gifting from God—something easy for you to do and that brings you joy, and that can bring joy to others.

"By doing these things for your neighbor you are doing them for God Himself . . ."

TELL ME WHAT YOU DO EVERY DAY, AND I WILL TELL YOU WHAT YOUR PRIORITIES ARE.

CHAPTER *Six*

THE POWER OF UNPLUGGING

MEDITATE

Why is it so important to take the time to unplug from the stressors of life? Why is it that stress is so powerful?

Stress alters the biochemistry of our body. It can be positive, or it can be negative. In a positive scenario, when we are presented with a life-threatening situation, our biology immediately goes into "fight, flight, or freeze" mode and begins to produce the hormones needed to survive immediate danger. We need that influx of cellular energy to run or to fight in order to protect ourselves and our loved ones. And, when we do, the hormone has served its purpose and our body retreats to normal cellular functions and rhythms.

However, in a negative scenario, when we have a constant state of low-grade stress due to daily living such as meeting deadlines, a toxic work environment, family drama, relational tension, financial stress, or constant exposure to social media and electronics, our body still produces the stress hormone, but we do not respond with life-threatening level speed to use the energy. Therefore, our biochemistry stores that energy in our body, which negatively impacts our health with responses like high blood pressure, weight gain,

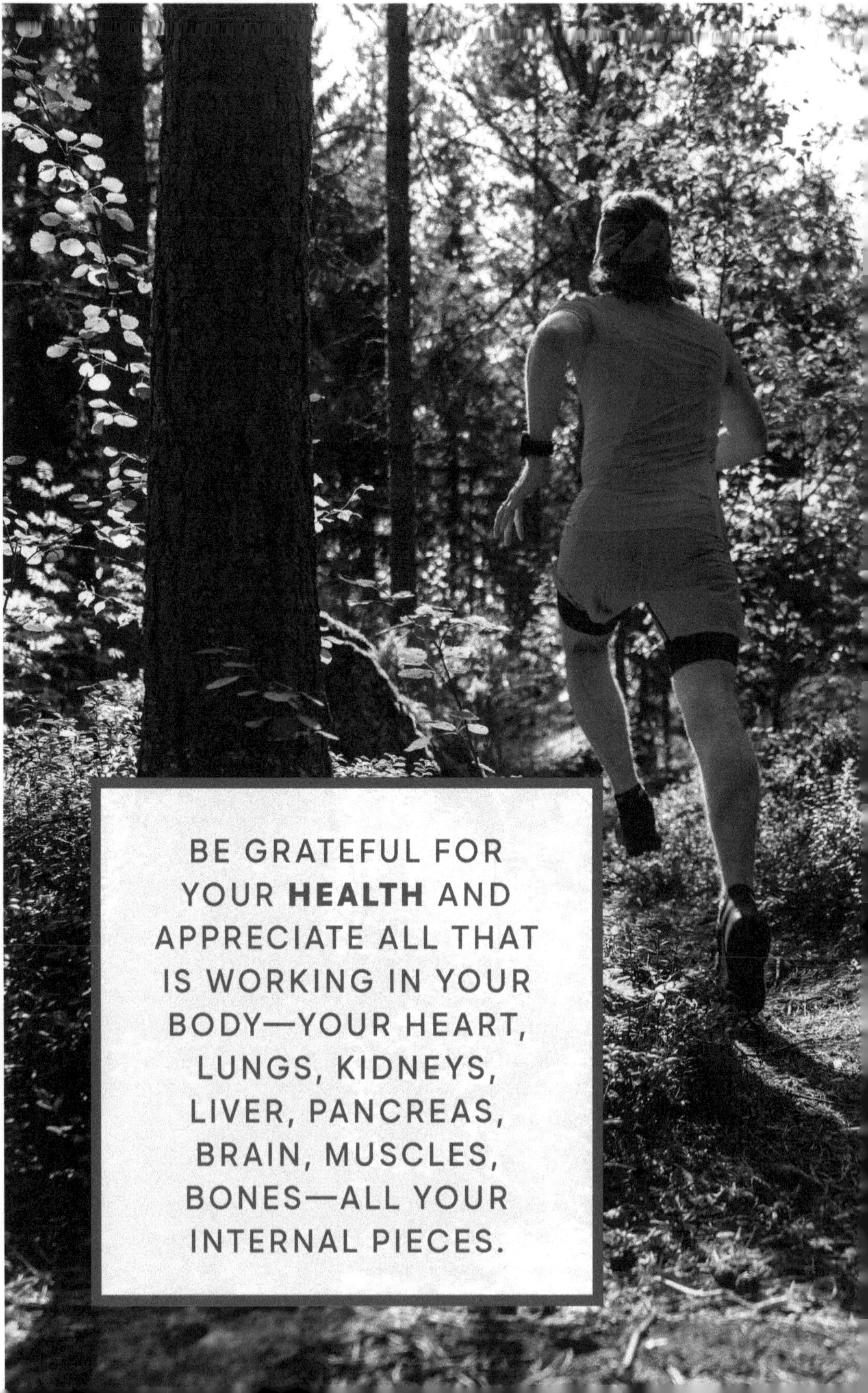

BE GRATEFUL FOR YOUR **HEALTH** AND APPRECIATE ALL THAT IS WORKING IN YOUR BODY—YOUR HEART, LUNGS, KIDNEYS, LIVER, PANCREAS, BRAIN, MUSCLES, BONES—ALL YOUR INTERNAL PIECES.

stress on organs, and more. Most of all, it impacts our mental health, and our access to peace, joy, and life energy.

How do we reduce and manage this daily stress? We need to stop, breathe, and reflect. Let's look at some simple ideas and tools to integrate into daily life routines. Let's also consider some ways we can unplug from our tech attachments. They, too, can exert their own form of stress-inducing influence on our lives.

ACTIVATE

Many times, when we "unplug" we don't quite know what to do with ourselves. We are so used to the stimulation of our devices and our stress. Here are some ideas for alternatives:

1. **Get on the move.** Walk, run, hike, shoot hoops, kick a soccer ball, exercise. (This will immediately change your biochemistry. And, it gives your mind a chance to think, reflect, and ponder healthy ways to address your stress.)
2. **Deep breathe.** Bring oxygen into your body—intentionally. Slow down and think about only the air you are breathing. Focus on only that one thing (yoga, meditation on scripture, etc.)
3. **Take a hot Epsom salt bath.** This changes biochemistry, and allows time to breathe and reflect. Turn off lights. Light candles. Inhale the fragrance.
4. **Take a hot sauna or steam bath.** This also changes biochemistry, and allows time to breathe and reflect. It is good for your skin and for your lungs.
5. **Listen to calming music.**
6. **Journal your thoughts and feelings.** Make a list of what you are grateful for.

7. **Engage in hands-on activities.** Break away from the cerebral and virtual activities of your electronics. Play a musical instrument, dig in the garden, build something, tinker with tools or wood, fix something, engage your physical skills and senses.
8. **Take the time to think about what you've been thinking about.** Replace negative thoughts with positive thoughts. Only use words in your mind that bring life to the situation.

RUMINATE

The power in unplugging from the stresses in life is that it allows the body to heal and recover, as well as establishes a healthy mindset to address the stress from a strong and healthy position in the future. You must choose a positive mindset to acquire a positive life. If you instead choose to stay in your stress, and to continue in negative thoughts and intentions, so will be the result of your reality and your future.

Choose to let go of that which you cannot control, or of what threatens to control you. Simply put: Let. It. Go.

Start where you are. Use what you have. Do what you can. When you turn off your devices, look around you and appreciate what you see. Appreciate what you hear. Appreciate what has been put before you. Be grateful for what you have both big and small—in your possessions, in your relationships, in your accomplishments, in your strengths, and even in areas where you need to grow. Spend time and thought in a place of pure gratitude.

Meditate AND *visualize* THE PLACES THAT BRING YOU JOY AND PEACE. IS IT THE MOUNTAINS? THE OCEAN? THE SANDY BEACH? WHATEVER OR WHEREVER IT IS, PUT YOURSELF RIGHT IN THE MIDDLE OF IT.

Remember, your cells respond to every thought:

- Good or bad
- Peaceful or stressful
- Blessing or curse
- Fight or flight

Therefore, keep your thoughts peaceful and positive.

Your *cells* respond to every thought . . .good or bad, peaceful or stressful, blessing or curse, fight or flight. Therefore, keep your thoughts *positive* about your body. Be intentional about every thought!

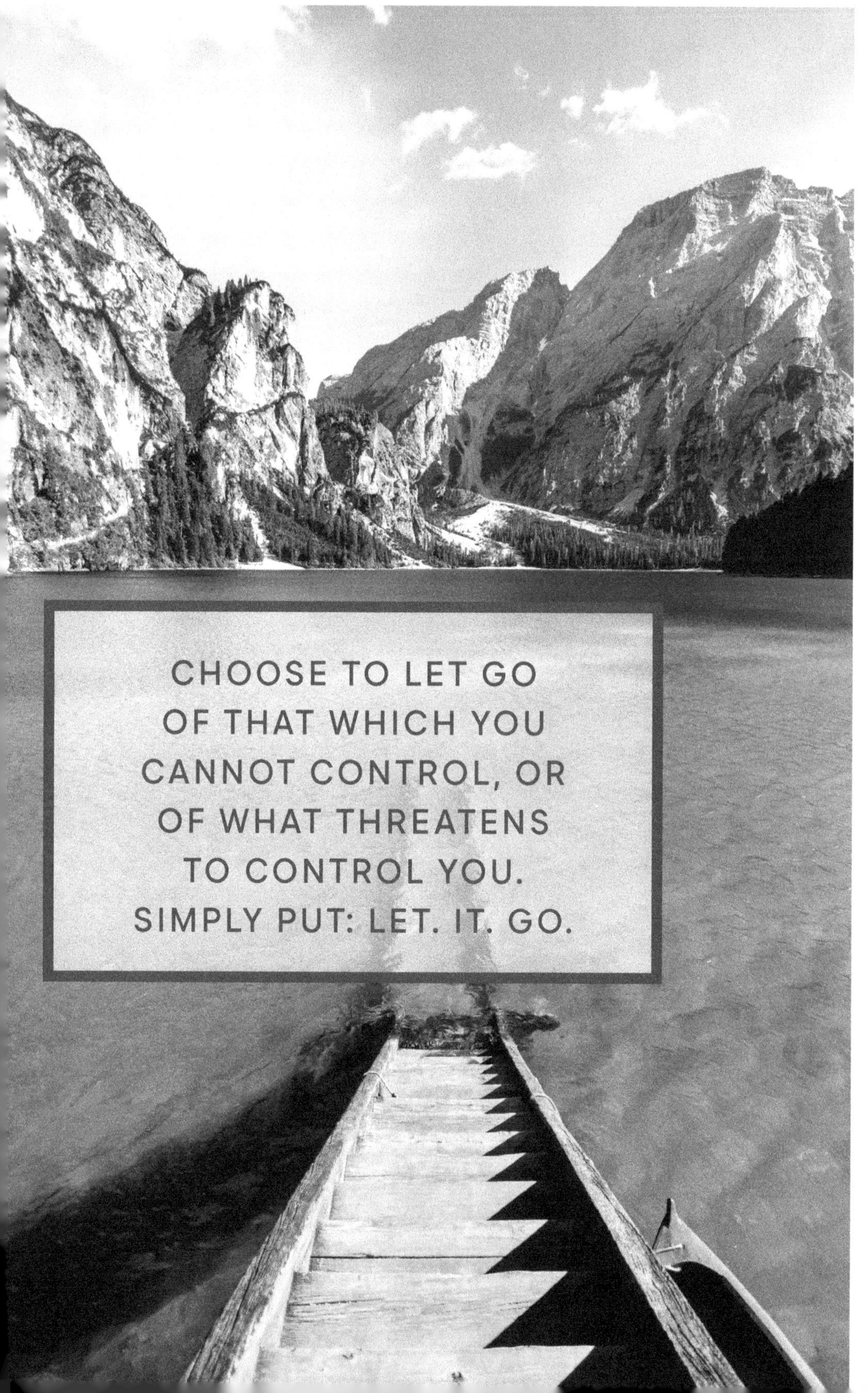

CHOOSE TO LET GO
OF THAT WHICH YOU
CANNOT CONTROL, OR
OF WHAT THREATENS
TO CONTROL YOU.
SIMPLY PUT: LET. IT. GO.

CHAPTER *Seven*

THE POWER OF SEEKING JOY

MEDITATE

Many religions and philosophies agree that what we seek, we find. Therefore, what we seek matters. Why is joy so powerful? Why is it important to have joy in your life?

There's research to prove that joy boosts our immune system, fights stress and pain, and improves our chance of living a longer life. Being authentically joyful could literally add years to your life! Joy is a great predictor of good health. Joyful people are kinder, healthier, and enjoy more meaningful relationships. Joyful people are more successful. Our brains work better in a positive state.

All we have is now. If we want to reclaim joy in living, we must seek joy today. Joy defined is "a feeling of great pleasure and happiness." Spiritually speaking, joy is a deeply rooted, inspired happiness. Joy is not automatic. People do not just say, "Oh, I think I want to have joy now," and *BOOM* it arrives at the front door. Alas, this it not how it works. Training our mind what to look for, what lens to see life through, takes practice.

Joy, in the deepest sense of the word, rises from the ashes, like a phoenix, from the suffering and loss of deep experiences. To know joy, one typically also knows suffering, grief, and loss. Joy—especially in the face of these obstacles—is truly intentional .

There are many books and articles on how to find joy and happiness in your life, and the good news is that they are easily accessible online. Just Google search it! What you will find is that there are many different angles and lenses with which to see joy, get joy, and practice joy. You can:

1. **See it.** I believe it starts with intention. We must put the lens of joy (*"How can I find joy in this?")* on every experience we encounter. Look for joy in the simile of a child, the presence of an animal, the beauty of a sunset, the power of a storm, etc.
2. **Speak it.** Once you can see joy, speak it. Verbally, out loud, express words that describe the joy . . .
   "That baby's smile screams joy!"
   "That child's laughter is pure joy!"
   "That sunset is God speaking joy and beauty to me and the world."
   "You bring me joy with your purring kitty."
3. **Do it.** After you speak words of joy, you will find your inner spirit starting to bubble. You may find your potential for busting out a big smile, and even laughter may prove evident. The next move is to take action When you feel the deep sense of joyful gratitude for life, it is time to be that joy to others. Be the joy!
   - Speak the beauty you see in that object.
   - Speak the gratitude you have for that object.
   - Speak blessing over the opportunity.
   - Smile and give a word of encouragement.
   - Be a blessing to that person or living creature through expression and intention.

4. **Achieve it.** Now take the time to reflect . . .
    - What brought you joy today?
    - Who brought you joy today?
    - Whose world did you bring joy to today?
    - Who and what was put before you today that provided you with an opportunity to *be* a blessing?

We need to recognize that we feed the fire of our heart. Some days it's difficult to lead with joy. Sometimes we are simply in a place where we need to sit with uncomfortable feelings and let them be—that is normal. However, we do have the power within us to move out of that place, when it is time. It is a balancing act.

How we respond to our circumstances in life is where we find our strength, and sometimes our weakness. Give yourself grace. We are on this journey that is far from perfect. We are continually in a state of becoming.

Seek Joy. Find Joy. And relish those moments before you.

See it. Speak it. Do it. Achieve it.

ACTIVATE

List *five* things you saw today (or yesterday) that brought you joy.

1. ______________________________
2. ______________________________
3. ______________________________
4. ______________________________
5. ______________________________

Which of these things, if any, did you actually *verbalize* out loud?

1. ______________________________
2. ______________________________
3. ______________________________
4. ______________________________
5. ______________________________

List *five* observations of joy that you spoke into another person's life today (or, that you could have, if you had seized the moment). If you missed it, don't be discouraged. The more you practice, the easier it will become.

1. ______________________________
2. ______________________________
3. ______________________________
4. ______________________________
5. ______________________________

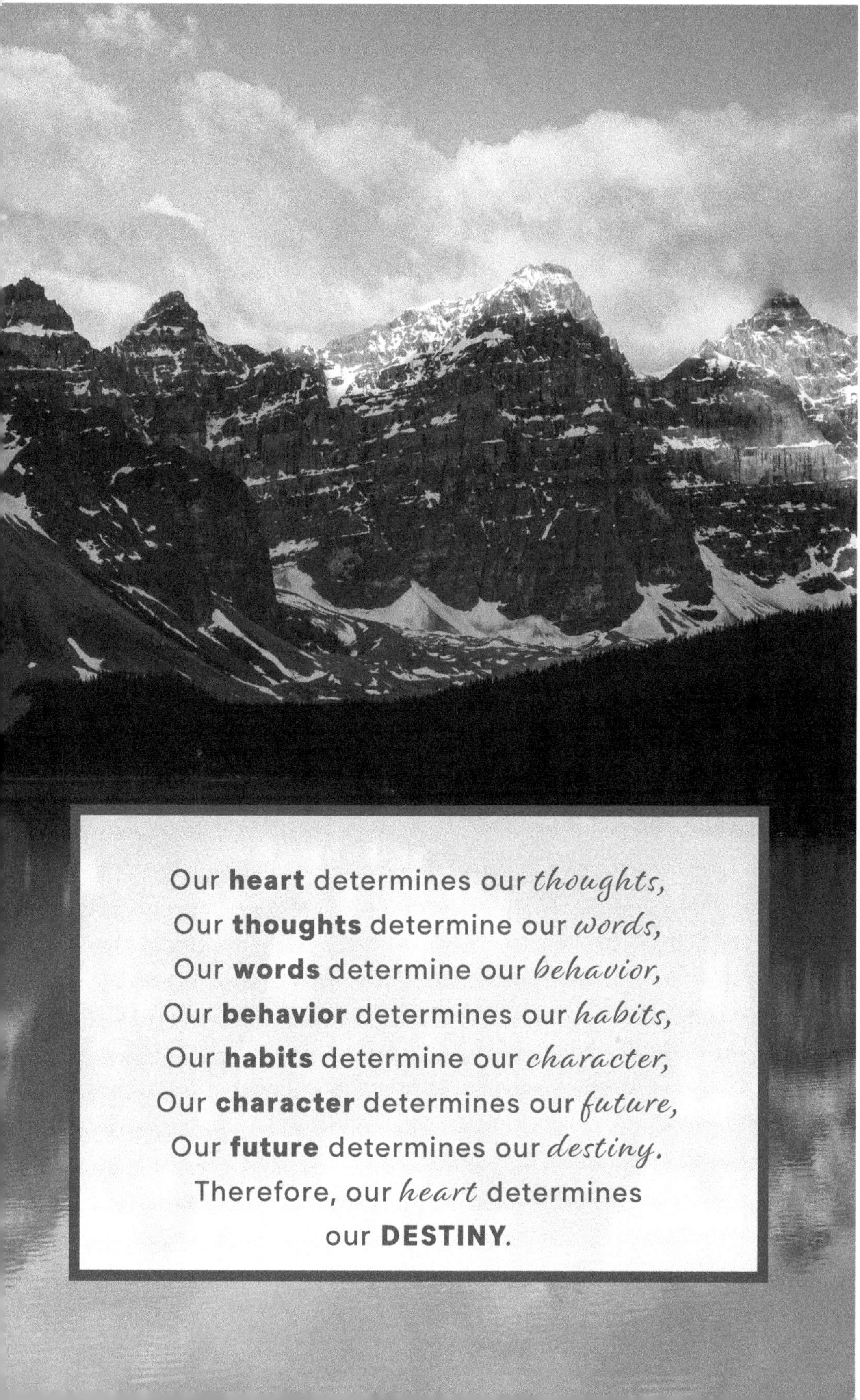

Our **heart** determines our *thoughts,*
Our **thoughts** determine our *words,*
Our **words** determine our *behavior,*
Our **behavior** determines our *habits,*
Our **habits** determine our *character,*
Our **character** determines our *future,*
Our **future** determines our *destiny.*
Therefore, our *heart* determines
our **DESTINY**.

RUMINATE

The following is a traditional Indian proverb:

> *One day a young boy was sitting with his elderly grandfather, and he asked him why it is so hard to do what is right. The grandfather listened. He then responded, "Sweet boy, in every man's heart there are two wolves. These wolves compete and fight to obtain power and control of the heart of every man. One wolf finds its strength in (hungers for) bitterness, anger, resentment, jealousy, and hate. The other wolf finds its strength in (hungers for) love, joy, peace, patience, kindness, and gentleness.*
>
> *The young boy listened. He then inquired, "Grandfather, this must be a strong battle. So, which wolf wins the competition for the power and control of the man's heart?"*
>
> *The grandfather paused, then whispered, "It is the one the man feeds."*

This story illustrates that there is power in what we feed our heart. We get to decide what we fill it with: in words, in morals, in values, in what we choose to read, in what we choose to watch, and in what emotion(s) we want to hold on to. Our heart determines our destiny and how we live our life to get there. Therefore, it is wise to intend on filling your heart with what is life-giving.

Imagine putting on the lens of God, and seeing the world and people through His eyes. God is love. God loves His creation. He sees the journey of each and every person and pours out love, grace, and blessing, even to the most difficult to love. He sees compassion and forgiveness; the most unlovable in the world, God loves wholly.

Authentic joy and true happiness are found in God's love:

- Read 1 Chronicles 16:27—Strength and joy fill His dwelling.
- Read Psalm 16:11—Joy and "eternal pleasures" are found in God's presence.

Read the references below with great care, and note how each one speaks to you:

"Deceit is in the heart of those who devise evil, but those who plan peace have joy." (Proverbs 12:20)

"Peace I leave with you; my peace I give to you . . . let your hearts not be troubled." (John 14:27)

"The fruit of the Spirit is love, joy, peace . . ." (Galatians 5:22)

CHAPTER *Eight*

THE POWER OF MINDFULNESS

Observe the present. Notice what's here, what's now. Be free of judging. Be free to feel. Breathe.

MEDITATE

The following quotes in this chapter come from many different theories, philosophies, and religions. Read with care and reflect how they speak to you, your life, and your experience.

"Mindful" is trendy. People use the word a lot. But how many truly practice mindfulness? I'm not sure of the statistics, but in my experience, I don't think it's the majority. Why? I believe it's because it requires us to slow down. People today are so busy being busy that the idea of stepping out of the rat race will destroy their chance of winning the prize.

Life is short. All we have is today, but we do have the power to control and determine our mindset and respond to the moment intentionally, on purpose, with an eternal focus:

- Love what is in front of you.
  People
  Creatures
  Opportunities
  Nature
  The Earth
  Yourself
- To fully love, we must gracefully acknowledge our imperfections and embrace a growth mindset to become the best we can be.
- Accept that we are not perfect, but we are doing our best to overcome our imperfections.
- When we can fully recognize that what we all share equally in this world is our unique imperfections, we can all accept and love one another—and ourselves—in our shared weaknesses and desire to grow.
- Be grateful for:
  Your health
  Your job
  Your family, Your friends
  Your faith
  The air you breathe
  Time
- Speak words of love, truth, and encouragement
- Be available
- Know your boundaries
- Verbally acknowledge what you see, hear, and experience.
- Be present

EMPTY SPACE IS A PLACE. NEITHER GIVE PLACE TO THE DEVIL (SEE EPHESIANS 4:27). AN EMPTY, PASSIVE MIND CAN BE EASILY FILLED WITH ALL KINDS OF WRONG THOUGHTS (SEE LUKE 11:24–26). YOU MUST IMMEDIATELY FILL SPACE THAT WAS ONCE OCCUPIED BY EVIL THOUGHTS WITH GOD'S WORDS AND GOD'S THOUGHTS.

You can change your thinking . . .
Difficult to do ~ YES
Impossible ~ NO
Patience, Persistence, Practice, and Perseverance.

A negative person is no fun to be with . . .
They bring a gloomy overcast to every project.
There is a heaviness about them.
They are a complainer,
A murmurer,
A fault-finder,
No matter how many good
Things are
Going on.

Face problems without making excuses for them.

Be a problem solver, not a problem maker.

See difficult situations as opportunities to grow, to be creative, to utilize your gifts and strengths.

God is constantly looking for someone to be gracious to, but it cannot be someone with a sour attitude and a negative mind (see Isaiah 30:18).

ACTIVATE

Appreciate what you have that works!

Your toes
Your legs
Your arms
Your core
Your hands
Your feet
Your head
Your neck
Your back
Your booty

Be grateful for a healthy:

Heart
Lungs
Kidneys
Liver
Pancreas
Brain
Muscles
Bones
All internal pieces

Focus on the Physical

Start your day with gratitude for the body you have—verbalize out loud how thankful you are for what you already have and what you desire for optimal health. Visualize yourself healthy and fit; see yourself as you want to be. Verbalize thanking God for what you see in your vision. Make affirmations out loud: "Thank you, Lord for showing me . . ." (whatever you see, whatever you want to gain in your physical health)

- I am healthy
- I am strong
- I am fit
- I am a Warrior for God

Say it out loud while you are moving your body; appreciate being in the moment.

Write your own affirmations below:

"A **PASSIVE** PERSON THINKS HE IS DOING NOTHING WRONG BECAUSE HE IS DOING *nothing* . . . (BUT) THE PROBLEM AROSE BECAUSE HE DID NOTHING."

—JOYCE MEYER

Be mindful of how you speak to your physical self and what you are grateful for. We, as women, tend to be very critical of our bodies. We see what is promoted by society and are paralyzed by a standard that is unachievable. Appreciate what you have in front of you and know that a healthy physical body is only as good as recognizing and honoring your present. Speak life into what you have right now. Speak life into what you can do right now. Appreciate what you have in front of you.

Using the practice of mindfulness, consider your own body. List five physical attributes and abilities you are grateful for:

1. ____________________
2. ____________________
3. ____________________
4. ____________________
5. ____________________

RUMINATE

Appreciate each and every moment, every breath . . . for it is God's gift. A new day, a new start, a new opportunity to be a blessing to someone, somewhere, somehow. This is what each day offers you. Be thankful for one more day to do something to please God, to honor Him with your life, and to build His Kingdom.

You harvest what you sow (Matthew 7:1-2). Do not judge or criticize or condemn others so that you may not be judged, criticized, and condemned yourself. Remember, do unto others just as you would have them do to you. Be mindful of what you speak into your attitude and perspective of today. Recognize that we only have today and what we sow into our daily choices impacts our tomorrow and what we harvest in the future. Therefore, embrace a healthy mindset!

Life is to be lived *here* and *now*. We are but a vapor in the wind, a wave tossed in the ocean. Make every breath and every action deliberate in every moment of every day. Remember: **passivity** is the opposite of *activity*. It is dangerous (see 1 Peter 1:5). We must be alert, cautious, and active.

CHAPTER *Nine*

THE POWER OF DAILY REFLECTION

MEDITATE

There is a power in reflection. At the end of the day, you can reflect on every opportunity put in front of you. How did you respond? How did you prioritize your time?

I believe there is no such thing as coincidence. Everything—every person, opportunity, conversation, bump in the road, discovery—is intentional. I believe that God is in control and allows for all of it, so that we can learn from it, grow from it, and sharpen our character. We have so much to learn about life here on Earth and who we are meant to be.

Therefore, it is imperative to take the time to reflect on *all* of it, every day. The Power of Reflection is in the growth of our character. The power is in how we can be even stronger tomorrow than we were yesterday. When we reflect, we can make different choices, use different words, choose different behavior. It allows us to repent, recover, renew, and re-do—whenever that bus comes around again. And, it allows us to build upon our strengths, our gifts, our gratitude, and our love from one another.

At the end of the day, after structured reflection, renewal begins.

Let's renew our life . . . starting today

"EXPECT
good
THINGS."
—JOYCE MEYER

ACTIVATE

The 4:8 Principle questions that are listed in Chapter 1 as well as in the next pages are used to structure both the beginning of the day (Daily Renewal) and Reflection at the end of the day. That's why I've included them at both the beginning and the end of this book. Take some time, now that you've completed this workbook, to ask yourself the same questions you did at the beginning. How have your answers changed?

I encourage you to do this every day: ask yourself the 4:8 Principle questions before you start your daily routine. Then, at the end of your day, ask them again as you reflect upon what you've experienced, from morning until night.

Ready. Set. Go!

Principle 4:8 Questions

1. What are *five* things I am thankful for right now?

____

____

____

____

____

2. What are *five* of my strengths or positive traits?

____

____

____

____

____

3. What are *five* of my best achievements so far?

4. What are *five* things I'm looking forward to in the next seven days?

RUMINATE

Every morning, I wake up and thank God for one more day. Each day is a chance to be a blessing to somebody and to make a positive impact in the world I live in. I may not know exactly who that person is, and that is okay. I will simply love on every person God puts in front of me! It may just be a smile, a compliment, an encouragement, a hug, a listening ear, or a heart of compassion. God knows exactly what others need, and a Spirit-filled nudge will direct my every move . . . at the right time.

And at the end of my day, upon reflection, I see God's hand all over every minute of it. I see that person I was to bring joy to, I see the creature to whom God said, "I see you," I see the area in my character that God said, "I am shaping

"DON'T LOSE **HOPE**
AND EMBRACE GUILT
WHEN YOU HAVE A
BAD DAY; JUST PICK
YOURSELF BACK UP,
DUST YOURSELF OFF,
AND START *again*."
–JOYCE MEYER

you, softening you, building you," and with joy and purpose in my heart, I am grateful for one more day.

Make it a GREAT DAY!
Be a blessing!
and
#SeekYourSunrise!

"When you fail, (not if), which we all do,
it does not mean *you* are a failure,
it just means you don't do everything
right the first time. Simply learn the lesson
and *try* again." **–JOYCE MEYER**

ACKNOWLEDGMENTS

Tami Carbone, this book and project would never have started without your incredible persistence to "just start writing." Your inspiration and belief in me is more than I had in myself. Thank you for that spirit. Thank you for just being you!

Amber Roller, thank you for allowing me to be your personal trainer and life coach in your journey to becoming a strong, healthy, confident woman as you approach your new chapter in life. Your trust in me, to be my very first client, is beyond words. Our journey is forever.

Lillian Amrine, my trusted colleague, friend, and typist . . .thank you for taking my jumbled document and putting it into legible form. You are an amazing woman, a trusted confidante, and a powerful sister in Christ!

Alexa Galena Martin, you are the most amazing life therapist. Thank you for your healing touch, your words of wisdom, and your always welcomed "Next Step" assignments. Your encouragement for me to finish the book and to believe in myself is unsurpassed. I adore you, sister!

ABOUT THE AUTHOR

Jennifer Clarke, M.Ed., has a passion to guide and encourage others to grow in their mindset and to seek and embrace a joy-filled, healthy life. Her faith and relationship with God drives her heart and her purpose.

Jen holds a B.A. in Psychology from the University of Washington, and a M.Ed. in Counseling K-12 from Seattle University. She is a Certified Life Coach through the Life Coach Institute of Orange County, and a Certified Personal Trainer and Nutrition Coach through the National Academy of Sports Medicine.

Jen is married to her high school sweetheart, Todd, and together they have raised their now-adult sons, Tyler and Hunter (and many critters), on their Fox Island, Washington homestead. The family enjoys running, hiking, SUP, skiing, mountain biking, and fitness, as well as summer evenings sitting around a bonfire recapturing the day's adventures.

After 25 years working in the high school and crisis counseling arena, Jen launched into her second career as a Personal Trainer and Health and Wellness Life Coach. This endeavor has unleashed a new spark in life and she has discovered a personal, joy-filled purpose that makes her DNA come ALIVE.

Jen's hope is that you will catch her passion and inspiration for health and joy and discover your own sense of purpose and fulfillment in the process, as you #seekyoursunrise, and experience your own *New Day, New Start!*

You can contact Jen at jen.clarke.fi@gmail.com.

With a strong, healthy body

You can be your best you!

You are fully alive to honor God

through using your gifts

to bring joy to others.

You bring joy to God by loving others,

with renewed energy,

which brings renewed

life!

CPSIA information can be obtained
at www.ICGtesting.com
Printed in the USA
BVHW090337221221
624588BV00010B/818

9 781952 943096